TO:

_____

FROM:

_____

3 MINUTES A DAY

EXTREME DEVOTIONS

FOR guys

Simon & Schuster, Inc.

NEW YORK   LONDON   TORONTO   SYDNEY

Simon & Schuster, Inc.

1230 Avenue of the Americas, New York, New York 10020

Scripture quotations are taken from:

Scriptures marked NIV® are from the *Holy Bible, New International Version*®. Copyright © 1973, 1978, 1984 by International Bible Society. Used by permission of Zondervan Publishing House. All rights reserved.

Scriptures marked NASB are taken from the *New American Standard Bible*®. Copyright © The Lockman Foundation 1960, 1962, 1963, 1968, 1971, 1972, 1973, 1975, 1977, 1995. Used by permission. (www.Lockman.org).

Scriptures marked NKJV are taken from the *New King James Version*®. Copyright © 1982 by Thomas Nelson, Inc. Used by permission. All rights reserved.

Scriptures marked NLT are taken from the *Holy Bible, New Living Translation*. Copyright © 1996. Used by permission of Tyndale House Publishers, Inc., Wheaton, Illinois 60189. All rights reserved.

Scriptures marked NCV are quoted from *The Holy Bible, New Century Version*. Copyright © 1987, 1988, 1991 by Word Publishing, Nashville, TN 37214. Used by permission.

Scriptures marked KJV are taken from the *King James Version*.

Scripture quotations marked MSG are taken from *The Message*. Copyright © by Eugene H. Peterson 1993, 1994, 1995. Used by permission of NavPress Publishing Group.

Scripture quotations marked ICB are taken from the *International Children's Bible, New Century Version*. Copyright © 1986, 1988 by Word Publishing, Nashville, TN 37214. Used by permission.

Scripture quotations marked TLB are taken from *The Living Bible* copyright © 1971. Used by permission of Tyndale House Publishers, Inc., Wheaton, Illinois 60189. All rights reserved.

Scripture quotations marked HCSB are taken from the *Holman Christian Standard Bible*®. Copyright © 1999, 2000, 2002, 2003 by Holman Bible Publishers. Used by permission. Holman Christian Standard Bible®, Holman CSB®, and HCSB® are federally registered trademarks of Holman Bible Publishers.

Cover Design by Kim Russell / Wahoo Designs
Page Layout by Bart Dawson

Manufactured in the United States of America

10 9 8 7 6 5 4 3 2 1

ISBN-13: 978-1-4169-1602-4
ISBN-10: 1-4169-1602-4

3 MINUTES A DAY

EXTREME DEVOTIONS

FOR *guys*

TABLE OF CONTENTS

INTRODUCTION

FACE facts: there was nothing middle-of-the-road about Jesus—He was extreme. He came to earth in an extremely unusual way. He made extreme claims; He did extreme things. And, He asked His followers to make extreme changes in their lives.

Now, here's the big question: Has Jesus made an extreme difference in your life, or are you satisfied to be a lukewarm believer who keeps Jesus at a "safe" distance? If you're determined to be a halfhearted Christian, then the idea of an extreme Jesus is probably a little bit unsettling, but if you desire to experience a more meaningful relationship with the One from Galilee, then the idea of following an extreme Jesus isn't very frightening at all.

This book can help you think about the extreme changes that Christ can make in your life. And the devotional readings are so short that you can probably read them in about three minutes. Can you spare three minutes a day for Jesus? Of course you can . . . and of course you should.

The text contains 31 devotional readings of particular interest to guys like you, busy guys who genuinely want to follow in the footsteps of Jesus. Each chapter contains Bible verses, a brief devotional reading, quotations from noted thinkers, and a prayer.

Are you willing make radical sacrifices for Jesus? If so, you may be certain of this fact: He's standing at the door of your heart, patiently waiting to form an extreme, life-altering relationship with you. Do you want to be a better person and a better Christian? If so, ask for God's help and ask for it many times each day . . . starting with a regular, heartfelt morning devotional. Even five minutes is enough time to change your day . . . and your life.

1

HOW EXTREME ARE YOU?

Don't look for shortcuts to God. The market is flooded with surefire, easygoing formulas for a successful life that can be practiced in your spare time. Don't fall for that stuff, even though crowds of people do. The way to life—to God!— is vigorous and requires total attention.

MATTHEW 7:13-14 MSG

JESUS made an extreme sacrifice for you. Are you willing to make extreme changes in your life for Him? Can you honestly say that you're passionate about your faith and that you're really following Jesus? Hopefully so. But if you're preoccupied with other things—or if you're strictly a one-day-a-week Christian—then you're in need of an extreme spiritual makeover!

Jesus doesn't want you to be a run-of-the-mill, follow-the-crowd kind of guy. Jesus wants you to be a "new creation" through Him. And that's exactly what you should want for yourself, too. Nothing is more important than your wholehearted commitment to your Creator and to His only begotten Son. Your faith must never be an afterthought; it must be your ultimate priority, your ultimate possession, and your ultimate passion.

You are the recipient of Christ's love. Accept it enthusiastically and share it passionately. Jesus deserves your extreme enthusiasm; the world deserves it; and you deserve the experience of sharing it.

THOUGHTS FOR TODAY

When we realize and embrace the Lord's
will for us, we will love to do it.
We won't want to do anything else.
It's a passion.

FRANKLIN GRAHAM

This is Christianity as God intended it—
a passionate, willful, and fully
emotional relationship.

BILL HYBELS

13

A TIP FOR TODAY

Be enthusiastic about your faith: John Wesley
wrote, " You don't have to advertise a fire. Get on
fire for God and the world will come to watch you
burn." When you allow yourself to become extremely enthusiastic about your faith, other people
will notice—and so will God.

A PRAYER FOR TODAY

Lord, let me find my strength in You.
When I am weary, give me rest.
When I feel overwhelmed,
let me look to You for my priorities.
Let Your passion be my passion, Lord,
and let Your way be my way,
today and forever.
Amen

14

EXTREME FAITH

*But without faith it is impossible to
please Him, for he who comes to God
must believe that He is, and that He is
a rewarder of those who diligently seek Him.*

HEBREWS 11:6 NKJV

ARE you a mountain-moving guy whose faith is evident for all to see? Or, are you a spiritual underachiever? As you think about the answer to that question, consider this: God needs more people who are willing to move mountains for His glory and for His kingdom.

Every life—including yours—is a series of wins and looses. Every step of the way, through every triumph and tragedy, God walks with you, ready and willing to strengthen you. So the next time you find your courage tested to the limit, remember to take your fears to God. If you call upon Him, you will be comforted. Whatever your challenge, whatever your trouble, God can handle it.

When you place your faith, your trust, indeed, your life in the hands of your Heavenly Father, you'll be amazed at the marvelous things He can do with you and through you. So strengthen your faith through praise, through worship, through Bible study, and through prayer. And trust God's plans. With Him, all things are possible, and He stands ready to open a world of possibilities to you . . . if you have faith.

And now, with no more delays, let the mountain moving begin.

THOUGHTS FOR TODAY

Faith is trusting in advance what will only make sense in reverse.

PHILLIP YANCEY

Only God can move mountains, but faith and prayer can move God.

E. M. BOUNDS

17

A TIP FOR TODAY

Faith Should Be Practiced More Than Studied. Vance Havner said, "Nothing is more disastrous than to study faith, analyze faith, make noble resolves of faith, but never actually to make the leap of faith." How true!

A PRAYER FOR TODAY

18

Lord, when it's difficult being
a Christian, give me the courage
and the wisdom to stand up
for my faith. Christ made
the ultimate sacrifice for me;
let me know stand up for Him!
Amen

3

SO MUCH TO DO; SO LITTLE TIME!

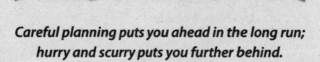

*Careful planning puts you ahead in the long run;
hurry and scurry puts you further behind.*

PROVERBS 21:5 MSG

TIME is a nonrenewable gift from God. But sometimes, we treat our time here on earth as if it were not a gift at all: We may be tempted to invest our lives in trivial pursuits and petty diversions. But our Father beckons each of us to a higher calling.

20

An important element of our stewardship to God is the way that we choose to spend the time He has entrusted to us. Each waking moment holds the potential to hug a child, or do a good deed, or say a kind word, or to offer a heartfelt prayer. Our challenge, as believers, is to use our time wisely in the service of God's work and in accordance with His plan for our lives.

Today, like every day, is a special treasure to be savored and celebrated. May we—as Christians who have so much to celebrate—never fail to praise our Creator by rejoicing in this glorious day . . . and by using it wisely.

THOUGHTS FOR TODAY

Our leisure, even our play, is a matter of
serious concern. There is no neutral ground
in the universe: every square inch,
every split second, is claimed by God
and counterclaimed by Satan.

C. S. LEWIS

The foe of opportunity is preoccupation.
Just when God sends along a chance to turn
a great victory for mankind, some of us are
too busy puttering around to notice it.

A. W. TOZER

A TIP FOR TODAY

Do first things first, and keep your focus on high-
priority tasks. And remember this: your highest priority should be your relationship with God and His
Son.

A PRAYER FOR TODAY

Dear Lord, when the demands
of the day leave me distracted and
discouraged, let me turn to Jesus for
the peace that only He can give.
And then, when I have accepted
the spiritual abundance that is mine
through Christ, let me share
His message and His love with all
who cross my path.
Amen

22

GOD HAS A PLAN . . . ARE YOU INTERESTED?

The Lord will work out his plans for my life—
for your faithful love, O Lord, endures forever.

PSALM 138:8 NLT

DO you think that God has big plans for you, or do you think that God wants you to be a do-nothing Christian? The answer should be obvious, but just for the record, here are the facts: 1. God has plans for your life that are far grander than you can imagine. 2. It's up to you to discover those plans and accomplish them . . . or not.

God has given you many gifts, including the gift of free will; that means that you have the ability to make choices and decisions on your own. The most important decision of your life is, of course, your commitment to accept Jesus Christ as your personal Lord and Savior. And once your eternal destiny is secured, you will undoubtedly ask yourself "What now, Lord?" If you earnestly seek God's plan for your life, you will find it…in time.

Sometimes, God's plans are crystal clear, but other times, He may lead you through the wilderness before He delivers you to the Promised Land. So be patient, keep praying, and keep seeking His will for your life. When you do, you'll be amazed at the marvelous things that an all-powerful, all-knowing God can do.

24

THOUGHTS FOR TODAY

**When you experience grace and are loved
when you do not deserve it, you spend
the rest of your life standing on tiptoes
trying to reach His plan for your life
out of gratitude.**

CHARLES STANLEY

25

**The one supreme business of life is to
find God's plan for your life and live it.**

E. STANLEY JONES

A TIP FOR TODAY

God has a wonderful plan for your life. And the time to start looking for that plan—and living it— is now. And remember—discovering God's plan begins with prayer.

A PRAYER FOR TODAY

Lord, You have a plan for my life.
Let me discover it and live it.
Today, I will seek Your will,
knowing that when I trust in You,
dear Father, I am eternally blessed.
Amen

5

PEER PRESSURE: POSITIVE OR NEGATIVE?

Don't become partners with those who reject God. How can you make a partnership out of right and wrong? That's not partnership; that's war. Is light best friends with dark?

2 CORINTHIANS 6:14 MSG

OUR world is filled with pressures: some good, some bad. The pressures that we feel to follow God's will and to obey His commandments are positive pressures. God places them on our hearts, and He intends that we act in accordance with these feelings. But we also face different pressures, ones that are definitely not from God. When we feel pressured to do things—or even to think thoughts—that lead us away from God, we must beware.

Rick Warren observed, "Those who follow the crowd usually get lost in it." We know these words to be true, but oftentimes we fail to live by them. Instead of trusting God for guidance, we imitate our friends and suffer the consequences. Instead of seeking to please our Father in heaven, we strive to please our peers, with decidedly mixed results. Instead of doing the right thing, we do the "easy" thing or the "popular" thing. And when we do, we pay a high price for our shortsightedness.

Are you satisfied to follow the crowd, or will you follow the One from Galilee? If you sincerely want to please God, you must resist the pressures that society seeks to impose upon you, and you must conform yourself, instead, to God's will, to His path, and to His Son.

28

THOUGHTS FOR TODAY

Fashion is an enduring testimony
to the fact that we live quite consciously
before the eyes of others.

JOHN ELDREDGE

If you try to be everything to everybody,
you will end up being nothing to anybody.

VANCE HAVNER

A TIP FOR TODAY

Face facts: since you can't please everybody, you're better off trying to please the people who are trying to help you become a better person, not the people who are encouraging you to misbehave!

A PRAYER FOR TODAY

Dear Lord, other people may
encourage me to stray from
Your path, but I wish to follow in
the footsteps of Your Son.
Give me the vision to see
the right path—and the wisdom
to follow it—today
and every day of my life.
Amen

30

6

TOO MUCH STUFF . . .

Keep your lives free from the love of money,
and be satisfied with what you have.

HEBREWS 13:5 NCV

"SO much stuff to shop for, and so little time . . ." These words seem to describe the priorities of our 21st-century world. Hopefully, you're not building your life around your next visit to the local mall—but you can be sure that many people are!

Our society is in love with money and the things that money can buy. God is not. God cares about people, not possessions, and so must we. We must, to the best of our abilities, love our neighbors as ourselves, and we must, to the best of our abilities, resist the mighty temptation to place possessions ahead of people.

Money, in and of itself, is not evil; worshipping money is. So today, as you prioritize matters of importance for you and yours, remember that God is almighty, but the dollar is not.

If we worship God, we are blessed. But if we worship "the almighty dollar," we are inevitably punished because of our misplaced priorities— and our punishment inevitably comes sooner rather than later.

32

THOUGHTS FOR TODAY

If you want to be truly happy, you won't find it
on an endless quest for more stuff.
You'll find it in receiving God's generosity
and then passing that generosity along.

BILL HYBELS

There is absolutely no evidence that complexity
and materialism lead to happiness.
On the contrary, there is plenty of evidence that
simplicity and spirituality lead to joy,
a blessedness that is better than happiness.

DENNIS SWANBERG

33

A TIP FOR TODAY

Stuff 101: The world says, "Buy more stuff." God says,
"Stuff isn't important." Believe God.

A PRAYER FOR TODAY

34

Heavenly Father, when I focus
intently upon You, I am blessed.
When I focus too intently on
the acquisition of material
possessions, I am troubled.
Make my priorities pleasing to You,
Father, and make me
a worthy servant of Your Son.
Amen

EXTREME GRATITUDE

*Everything created by God is good,
and nothing is to be rejected, if it is received
with gratitude; for it is sanctified by means of
the word of God and prayer.*

1 TIMOTHY 4:4-5 NASB

IF you're like most guys on the planet, you're a very busy fellow. Your life is probably hectic, demanding, and complicated. When the demands of life leave you rushing from place to place with scarcely a moment to spare, you may fail to pause and thank your Creator for the blessings He has bestowed upon you. Big mistake.

36

No matter how busy you are, you should never be too busy to thank God for His gifts. Your task, as an extreme follower of the living Christ, is to praise God many times each day. After all, your Heavenly Father has blessed you beyond measure, and you owe Him everything, including your thanks, starting now.

THOUGHTS FOR TODAY

Thanksgiving is good but Thanksliving is better.

JIM GALLERY

The words "thank" and "think" come from
the same root word. If we would think more,
we would thank more.

WARREN WIERSBE

37

A TIP FOR TODAY

When is the best time to say "thanks" to God? Any
Time. God never takes a vacation, and He's always
ready to hear from you. So what are you waiting
for?

A PRAYER FOR TODAY

38

Dear Lord, I am a very lucky guy,
and I thank You for my blessings.
Help me to be a good person,
and help me use my talents
and my possessions for Your Glory ...
and for Your Son.
Amen

EXTREME FAMILIARITY WITH YOUR BIBLE

But He answered, "It is written:
Man must not live on bread alone,
but on every word that comes
from the mouth of God."

MATTHEW 4:4 HCSB

DO you read your Bible a lot . . . or not?
The answer to this simple question will determine, to a surprising extent, the quality of your life and the direction of your faith.

As you establish priorities for life, you must decide whether God's Word will be a bright spotlight that guides your path every day or a tiny nightlight that occasionally flickers in the dark. The decision to study the Bible—or not—is yours and yours alone. But make no mistake: how you choose to use your Bible will have a profound impact on you and your loved ones.

40

The Bible is unlike any other book. It is a priceless gift from your Creator, a tool that God intends for you to use in every aspect of your life. And, it contains promises upon which you, as a Christian, can and must depend.

Jonathan Edwards advised, "Be assiduous in reading the Holy Scriptures. This is the fountain whence all knowledge in divinity must be derived. Therefore let not this treasure lie by you neglected."

God's Holy Word is, indeed, a priceless, one-of-a-kind treasure. Handle it with care, but more importantly, handle it every day.

THOUGHTS FOR TODAY

Nobody ever outgrows Scripture;
the book widens and deepens with our years.

C. H. SPURGEON

God announced Himself with
an exclamation mark by proclaiming
His nature in a type of autobiography,
a book called the Bible.

41

BILL HYBELS

A TIP FOR TODAY

It's up to you: Nobody can study the Bible for you
. . . you've got to study it for yourself. And that's exactly what you should do.

A PRAYER FOR TODAY

Dear Lord, the Bible is Your gift to me.
Let me use it, let me trust it,
and let me obey it,
today and every day that I live.
Amen

42

9

EXTREME DISCIPLINE

But I discipline my body and bring it into subjection, lest, when I have preached to others, I myself should become disqualified.

1 CORINTHIANS 9:27 NKJV

ARE you a self-disciplined guy? If so, congratulations . . . if not, God wants to have a little talk with you.

God doesn't reward laziness, misbehavior, or apathy. To the contrary, He expects His followers to behave with dignity and discipline. But sometimes, it's extremely difficult to be dignified and disciplined. Why? Because the world wants us to believe that dignified, self-disciplined behavior is going out of style.

44

You live in a world in which leisure is glorified and indifference is often glamorized. But God has other plans. He did not create you to be ordinary; He created you for far greater things.

Face facts: Life's greatest rewards aren't likely to fall into your lap. To the contrary, your greatest accomplishments will probably require lots of work, which is perfectly fine with God. After all, He knows that you're up to the task, and He has big plans for you. God will do His part to fulfill those plans, and the rest, of course, is up to you.

THOUGHTS FOR TODAY

**If one examines the secret behind
a championship football team,
a magnificent orchestra, or a successful
business, the principal ingredient is
invariably discipline.**

JAMES DOBSON

**Simply stated, self-discipline is obedience
to God's Word and willingness to submit
everything in life to His will,
for His ultimate glory.**

JOHN MACARTHUR

A TIP FOR TODAY

Discipline is not a four-letter word: Exercising discipline should never be viewed as an imposition or as a form of punishment; far from it. Discipline is the means by which you can take control of your life (which, by the way, is far better than letting your life control you).

A PRAYER FOR TODAY

Lord, I want to be a disciplined
believer. Let me use my time wisely,
and let me teach others by
the faithfulness of my conduct,
today and every day.
Amen

EXTREMELY WISE

Those who are wise will shine like the brightness of the heavens, and those who lead many to righteousness, like the stars forever and ever.

DANIEL 12:3 NIV

ARE you a wise guy? Hopefully, you're a very wise fellow who's getting wiser every day. But even if you're a very smart fellow, there's still lots more for you to learn.

Wisdom is not like a dandelion or a mushroom; it does not spring up overnight. It is, instead, like an oak tree that starts as a tiny acorn, grows into a sapling, and eventually reaches up to the sky, tall and strong. To become wise, you must seek God's wisdom and live according to His Word. To become wise, you must seek wisdom with consistency and purpose. To become wise, you must not only learn the lessons of the Christian life; you must also live by them.

48

Are you passionate in your pursuit of God's wisdom? And do you sincerely seek to live a life of righteousness? If so, you must study the ultimate source of wisdom: the Word of God. You must seek out worthy teachers and listen carefully to their advice. You must associate, day in and day out, with godly friends. And, you must act in accordance with your beliefs. When you do these things, you will become wise . . . and you will be a blessing to your friends, to your family, and to the world.

THOUGHTS FOR TODAY

There are some things that can be learned
by the head, but Christ crucified
can only be learned by the heart.

C. H. SPURGEON

Don't expect wisdom to come into your life
like great chunks of rock on a conveyor belt.
Wisdom comes privately from God as
a byproduct of right decisions, godly reactions,
and the application of spiritual principles
to daily circumstances.

CHARLES SWINDOLL

49

A TIP FOR TODAY

Wisdom in Proverbs: If you're looking for wisdom,
the Book of Proverbs is a wonderful place to start.
It has 31 chapters, one for each day of the month.
If you read Proverbs regularly, and if you take its
teachings to heart, you'll gain timeless wisdom
from God's unchanging Word.

A PRAYER FOR TODAY

50

Lord, when I trust in the wisdom
of the world, I will sometimes be led
astray, but when I trust in
Your wisdom, I build my life on
a firm foundation. Today and
every day I will trust Your Word
and follow it, knowing that
the ultimate wisdom is Your wisdom
and the ultimate truth is Your truth.
Amen

EXTREME KINDNESS

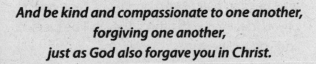

And be kind and compassionate to one another,
forgiving one another,
just as God also forgave you in Christ.

EPHESIANS 4:32 HCSB

KINDNESS is a choice. Sometimes, when we feel happy or generous, we find it easy to be kind. Other times, when we are discouraged or tired, we can scarcely summon the energy to utter a single kind word. But, God's commandment is clear: He intends that we make the conscious choice to treat others with kindness and respect, no matter our circumstances, no matter our emotions.

In the busyness and confusion of daily life, it is easy to lose focus, and it is easy to become frustrated. We are imperfect human beings struggling to manage our lives as best we can, but we often fall short. When we are distracted or disappointed, we may neglect to share a kind word or a kind deed. This oversight hurts others, but it hurts us most of all.

Today, slow yourself down and be alert for people who need your smile, your kind words, or your helping hand. Make kindness a centerpiece of your dealings with others. They will be blessed, and you will be, too.

52

THOUGHTS FOR TODAY

**When you launch an act of kindness
out into the crosswinds of life,
it will blow kindness back to you.**

DENNIS SWANBERG

**When you extend hospitality to others,
you're not trying to impress people,
you're trying to reflect God to them.**

MAX LUCADO

A TIP FOR TODAY

You can't just talk about it: In order to be a kind person, you must do kind things. Thinking about them isn't enough. So get busy! The day to start being a more generous person is today!

53

A PRAYER FOR TODAY

Dear Lord, help me see the needs of those around me. Today, let me spread kind words of thanksgiving and celebration in honor of Your Son. Let forgiveness rule my heart, and let my love for Christ be reflected through the acts of kindness that I extend to those who need the healing touch of the Master's hand. Amen

54

12

EXTREME FORGIVENESS

Then Peter came to him and asked,
"Lord, how often should I forgive someone
who sins against me? Seven times?"
"No!" Jesus replied, "seventy times seven!

MATTHEW 18:21-22 NLT

FORGIVING other people is hard—sometimes very hard. But God tells us that we must forgive others, even when we'd rather not. So, if you're angry with anybody (or if you're upset by something you yourself have done) it's time to forgive . . . now!

Life would be much simpler if you could forgive people "once and for all" and be done with it. Yet forgiveness is seldom that easy. Usually, the decision to forgive is straightforward, but the process of forgiving is more difficult. Forgiveness is a journey that requires effort, time, perseverance, and prayer.

God instructs you to treat other people exactly as you wish to be treated. And since you want to be forgiven for the mistakes that you make, you must be willing to extend forgiveness to other people for the mistakes that they have made. If you can't seem to forgive someone, you should keep asking God to help you until you do. And you can be sure of this: if you keep asking for God's help, He will give it.

56

THOUGHTS FOR TODAY

Looking back over my life, all I can see is mercy and grace written in large letters everywhere. May God help me have the same kind of heart toward those who wound or offend me.

JIM CYMBALA

The well of God's forgiveness never runs dry.

57

GRADY NUTT

A TIP FOR TODAY

What if it's really difficult to forgive somebody? If forgiveness were easy, everybody would be doing it—but it's not always easy to forgive and forget. If you simply can't seem to forgive someone, start praying about it . . . and keep praying about it . . . until God helps you do the right thing.

A PRAYER FOR TODAY

Lord, just as You have forgiven me,
I am going to forgive others.
When I forgive others, I not only obey
Your commandments, but I also free
myself from bitterness and regret.
Forgiveness is Your way, Lord,
and I will make it my way, too.
Amen

58

13

SETTING AN EXTREMELY GOOD EXAMPLE

You should be an example to the believers in speech, in conduct, in love, in faith, in purity.

1 TIMOTHY 4:12 HCSB

OKAY, here's a question: What kind of example are you? Are you the kind of guy whose life serves as a powerful example of decency and morality? Are you a guy whose behavior serves as a positive role model for others? Are you the kind of guy whose actions, day in and day out, are based upon integrity, fidelity, and a love for the Lord? If so, you are not only blessed by God, but you are also a powerful force for good in a world that desperately needs positive influences such as yours.

60

We live in a dangerous, temptation-filled world. That's why you encounter so many opportunities to stray from God's commandments. Resist those temptations! When you do, you'll earn God's blessings, and you'll serve as positive role model for your family and friends.

Phillips Brooks advised, "Be such a man, and live such a life, that if every man were such as you, and every life a life like yours, this earth would be God's Paradise." And that's sound advice because our families and friends are watching . . . and so, for that matter, is God.

THOUGHTS FOR TODAY

Our walk counts far more than our talk, always!

GEORGE MUELLER

A holy life will produce the deepest impression.
Lighthouses blow no horns;
they only shine.

D. L. MOODY

61

A TIP FOR TODAY

Living your life and shining your light . . . As a Christian, the most important light you shine is the light that your own life shines on the lives of others. May your light shine brightly, righteously, obediently, and eternally!

A PRAYER FOR TODAY

Lord, make me a worthy example
to my family and friends.
And, let my words and my deeds
serve as a testimony to the changes
You have made in my life.
Let me praise You, Father,
by following in the footsteps
of Your Son, and let others see
Him through me.
Amen

62

14

THERE'S WORK TO DO!

In all the work you are doing,
work the best you can. Work as if you were
doing it for the Lord, not for people.

COLOSSIANS 3:23 NCV

HAVE you acquired the habit of doing first things first, or are you one of those guys who put off important work until the last minute? The answer to this simple question will help determine how well you do your work and how much fun you have doing it.

God's Word teaches us the value of hard work. In his second letter to the Thessalonians, Paul warns, " ...if any would not work, neither should he eat" (3:10 KJV). And the Book of Proverbs proclaims, "One who is slack in his work is brother to one who destroys" (18:9 NIV). In short, God has created a world in which diligence is rewarded and laziness is not. So, whatever it is that you choose to do, do it with commitment, excitement, and vigor. And remember this: Hard work is not simply a proven way to get ahead; it's also part of God's plan for you.

64

THOUGHTS FOR TODAY

It may be that the day of judgment
will dawn tomorrow; in that case,
we shall gladly stop working for
a better tomorrow. But not before.

DIETRICH BONHOEFFER

65

If you want to reach your potential,
you need to add a strong work ethic
to your talent.

JOHN MAXWELL

A TIP FOR TODAY

Wherever you happen to be, be the best you can
be: Giving your best is habit-forming, so give your
best every time you go to work.

A PRAYER FOR TODAY

Lord, let me be an industrious worker
in Your fields. Those fields are ripe,
Lord, and Your workers are few.
Let me be counted as Your faithful,
diligent servant today, and every day.
Amen

YOUR PRIORITIES AND GOD'S . . . HOW SIMILAR ARE THEY?

The thing you should want most is God's kingdom and doing what God wants. Then all these other things you need will be given to you.

MATTHEW 6:33 NCV

HERE'S a quick quiz: Whose expectations are you trying to meet?

A. Your friends' expectations

B. Society's expectations

C. God's expectations

If you're a Christian, the correct answer is C., but if you're overly concerned with either A. or B., you're not alone. Plenty of guys invest too much energy trying to meet society's expectations and too little energy trying to please God. It's a common behavior, but it's also a very big mistake.

A better strategy, of course, is to try to please God first. To do so, you must prioritize your day according to God's commandments, and you must seek His will and His wisdom in all matters. Then, you can face each day with the assurance that the same God who created our universe out of nothingness will help you place first things first in your own life.

Are you having trouble choosing between God's priorities and society's priorities? Are you feeling overwhelmed or confused? If so, turn the concerns over to God—prayerfully, earnestly, and often. Then, listen for His answer . . . and trust the answer He gives.

THOUGHTS FOR TODAY

Whatever you love most, be it sports, pleasure, business or God, that is your god.

BILLY GRAHAM

Don't take hold of a thing
unless you want that thing
to take hold of you.

69

E. STANLEY JONES

A TIP FOR TODAY

Make God a priority: Your days are probably filled to the brim with lots of obligations. But remember: no obligation is greater than the debt you owe to your Creator. So make sure that you give Him the time He deserves, not only on Sundays, but also on every other day of the week.

A PRAYER FOR TODAY

Dear Lord, make me a person of
unwavering commitment to You,
to my family, and to my friends.
Guide me away from the temptations
and distractions of this world,
so that I might honor You with
my thoughts, my actions,
and my prayers.
Amen

TOO BUSY TO PRAY?

*Then if my people who are called by
my name will humble themselves
and pray and seek my face and turn from their
wicked ways, I will hear from heaven and
will forgive their sins and heal their land.*

2 CHRONICLES 7:14 NLT

OKAY, from the looks of things, you're an extremely busy guy. And perhaps, because of your demanding schedule, you've neglected to pay sufficient attention to a particularly important part of your life: the spiritual part. If so, today is the day to change, and one way to make that change is simply to spend a little more time talking with God.

God is trying to get His message through to you. Are you listening?

Perhaps, on occasion, you may find yourself overwhelmed by the press of everyday life. Perhaps you may forget to slow yourself down long enough to talk with God. Instead of turning your thoughts and prayers to Him, you may rely upon your own resources. Instead of asking God for guidance, you may depend only upon your own limited wisdom. A far better course of action is this: simply stop what you're doing long enough to open your heart to God; then listen carefully for His directions.

In all things great and small, seek God's wisdom and His grace. He hears your prayers, and He will answer. All you must do is ask.

72

THOUGHTS FOR TODAY

The most powerful life is the most simple life.
The most powerful life is the life that knows
where it's going, that knows where the source of
strength is; it is the life that stays free of clutter
and happenstance and hurriedness.

MAX LUCADO

73

I have heard some Christians say,
"I do not feel in a proper frame of mind to pray."
My brother, then pray until you do.

C. H. SPURGEON

A TIP FOR TODAY

Prayer strengthens your relationship with God . . .
so pray. D. L. Moody observed, "The Christian on his
knees sees more than the philosopher on tiptoe."
It's up to you to live—and pray—accordingly.

A PRAYER FOR TODAY

Dear Lord, let me raise my hopes and
my dreams, my worries and my fears
to You. Let me be a worthy example to
74   family and friends, showing them
the importance and the power of
prayer. Let me take everything to
You in prayer, Lord, and when I do,
let me trust in Your answers.

Amen

DOING WHAT'S RIGHT

*Are there those among you who are truly wise
and understanding? Then they should show it
by living right and doing good things
with a gentleness that comes from wisdom.*

JAMES 3:13 NCV

OKAY, answer this question honestly: Do you behave differently because of your relationship with Jesus, or do you behave in pretty much the same way that you would if you weren't a believer? Hopefully, the fact that you've invited Christ to reign over your heart means that you've made extreme changes in your thoughts and your actions.

76

Doing the right thing is not always easy, especially when you're tired or frustrated. But, doing the wrong thing almost always leads to trouble. And sometimes, it leads to big trouble.

If you're determined to follow "the crowd," you may soon find yourself headed in the wrong direction. So here's some advice: Don't follow the crowd—follow Jesus. And keep following Him every day of your life.

THOUGHTS FOR TODAY

What is God looking for?
He is looking for men and women
whose hearts are completely His.

CHARLES SWINDOLL

Learning God's truth and getting it
into our heads is one thing, but living God's
truth and getting it into our characters is
quite something else.

WARREN WIERSBE

A TIP FOR TODAY

If you're not sure that it's the right thing to do, don't
do it! And if you're not sure that it's the truth, don't
tell it.

A PRAYER FOR TODAY

78

Lord, Your laws are perfect;
let me live by those laws.
And, let my life be an example for
others to follow so that they, too,
might come to know the everlasting
love of Your Son Jesus.
Amen

18

EXTREME PERSEVERANCE

Keep your eyes open,
hold tight to your convictions,
give it all you've got, be resolute.

1 CORINTHIANS 16:13 MSG

ARE you one of those guys who doesn't give up easily, or are you quick to bail out when the going gets tough? If you've developed the unfortunate habit of giving up at the first sign of trouble, it's probably time for you to have a heart-to-heart talk with the guy you see every time you look in the mirror.

A well-lived life is like a marathon, not a sprint—it calls for preparation, determination, and lots of perseverance. As an example of perfect perseverance, you need look no further than your Savior, Jesus Christ.

Jesus finished what He began. Despite His suffering and despite the shame of the cross, Jesus was steadfast in His faithfulness to God. You, too, should remain faithful, especially when times are tough.

Are you facing a difficult situation? If so, remember this: whatever your problem, God can handle it. Your job is to keep persevering until He does.

80

THOUGHTS FOR TODAY

Keep adding, keep walking, keep advancing;
do not stop, do not turn back,
do not turn from the straight road.

ST. AUGUSTINE

I learned as never before that persistent calling
upon the Lord breaks through every stronghold
of the devil, for nothing is impossible with God.
For Christians in these troubled times,
there is simply no other way.

JIM CYMBALA

81

A TIP FOR TODAY

The world encourages instant gratification, but
God's work usually takes time. Remember the
words of C. H. Spurgeon: "By perseverance, the
snail reached the ark."

A PRAYER FOR TODAY

Lord, some days I feel like there's
no way I can win. But when I'm
discouraged, let me turn to You for
strength, courage, and faith.
When I find my strength in You,
Lord, I am protected,
today and forever.
Amen

82

FOLLOWING IN THOSE EXTREME FOOTSTEPS

Keep your eyes on Jesus, who both began and finished this race we're in. Study how he did it. Because he never lost sight of where he was headed—that exhilarating finish in and with God—he could put up with anything along the way: cross, shame, whatever. And now he's there, in the place of honor, right alongside God.

HEBREWS 12:2 MSG

WHOM will you walk with today? Will you walk with people who worship the ways of the world? Or will you walk with the Son of God?

Jesus walks with you. Are you walking with Him? Hopefully, you will choose to walk with Him today and every day of your life.

Jesus has called upon believers of every generation (and that includes you) to follow in His footsteps. And God's Word promises that when you follow in Christ's footsteps, you will learn how to live freely and lightly (Matthew 11:28-30).

Are you worried about the day ahead? Be confident in God's power. He will never desert you. Are you concerned about the future? Be courageous and call upon God. He will protect you. Are you confused? Listen to the quiet voice of your Heavenly Father. He is not a God of confusion. Talk with God; listen to Him; follow His commandments . . . and walk with His Son— starting now.

THOUGHTS FOR TODAY

If you'll flip from cover to cover, you'll notice
that it's overwhelmingly a book of stories—
tales of men and women who walked with God.

JOHN ELDREDGE

Our responsibility is to feed from Him,
to stay close to Him, to follow Him—
because sheep easily go astray—so that we
eternally experience the protection
and companionship of our Great Shepherd
the Lord Jesus Christ.

FRANKLIN GRAHAM

A TIP FOR TODAY

Following Christ is a daily journey: When you decide to walk in the footsteps of the Master, that
means that you're agreeing to be a disciple seven
days a week, not just on Sundays.

A PRAYER FOR TODAY

Dear Lord, help me become the man
I can be and should be.
Guide me along a path of
Your choosing, and let me follow
in the footsteps of Your Son,
today and every day.
Amen

86

20

EXTREME TEMPTATION

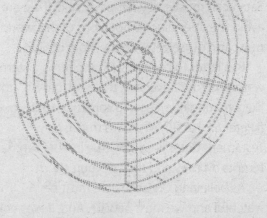

Then Jesus told him, "Go away, Satan! For it is written: You must worship the Lord your God, and you must serve Him only."

MATTHEW 4:10 HCSB

WE live in a world filled with an extreme number of temptations. The devil is working overtime causing pain and heartache in more places and in more ways than ever before. We, as followers of Christ, must remain vigilant. Not only must we resist Satan when he confronts us, but we must also avoid those places where Satan can most easily tempt us. And, if we are to avoid the unending temptations of this world, we must arm ourselves with the Word of God.

In a letter to believers, Peter offered a stern warning: "Your adversary, the devil, prowls around like a roaring lion, seeking someone to devour" (I Peter 5:8 NASB). What was true in New Testament times is equally true in our own. Satan tempts his prey and then devours them.

As believing Christians, we must be watchful and we must beware. And, if we seek righteousness in our own lives, we must earnestly wrap ourselves in the protection of God's Holy Word. When we do, we are protected.

THOUGHTS FOR TODAY

Rebuke the Enemy in your own name
and he laughs; command him in the name
of Christ and he flees.

JOHN ELDREDGE

If you don't avoid the bait . . .
you'll end up on the hook.

ANONYMOUS

89

A TIP FOR TODAY

Pray a little more: If life's inevitable temptations seem to be getting the best of you, try praying more often, even if many of those prayers are simply brief, "open-eyed" requests to your Father in heaven.

A PRAYER FOR TODAY

Lord, temptation is everywhere!
Help me turn from it and to run
from it! Let me keep Christ in
my heart, and let me put the devil
in his place: far away from me!
Amen

21

MAKING THE MOST OF YOUR EXTREME TALENTS

God has given gifts to each of you from his great variety of spiritual gifts. Manage them well so that God's generosity can flow through you.

1 PETER 4:10 NLT

ALL of us have special talents, and you are no exception. But your talent is no guarantee of success; it must be cultivated and nurtured; otherwise, it will go unused…and God's gift to you will be squandered.

92

Your particular talent is an extremely valuable treasure on temporary loan from God. He intends that you use your talent to enrich the world and to enrich your own life. Value the gift that God has given you, nourish it, make it grow, and share it with the world. Starting now!

THOUGHTS FOR TODAY

In the great orchestra we call life,
you have an instrument and a song,
and you owe it to God to
play them both sublimely.

MAX LUCADO

You are the only person on earth
who can use your ability.

ZIG ZIGLAR

A TIP FOR TODAY

Converting talent into skill requires work: Remember the old adage: "What we are is God's gift to us; what we become is our gift to God."

A PRAYER FOR TODAY

94

Lord, You gave me talents and abilities
for a reason. Let me use my talents
for the glory of Your kingdom,
and let me praise You always
because You are the Giver of all gifts,
including mine.
Amen

22

SHARING YOUR FAITH

But when the Holy Spirit has come upon you,
you will receive power and will tell people about
me everywhere—in Jerusalem, throughout
Judea, in Samaria, and to the ends of the earth.

ACTS 1:8 NLT

OUR personal testimonies are extremely important, but sometimes, because of shyness or insecurities, we're afraid to share our experiences. And that's unfortunate.

In his second letter to Timothy, Paul shares a message to believers of every generation when he writes, "God has not given us a spirit of timidity" (1:7). Paul's meaning is clear: When sharing our beliefs, we, as Christians, must be courageous, forthright, and unashamed.

Billy Graham observed, "Our faith grows by expression. If we want to keep our faith, we must share it." If you are a follower of Christ, the time to express your belief in Him is now. You know how He has touched your heart; help Him do the same for others.

THOUGHTS FOR TODAY

Nothing else you do will ever matter
as much as helping people establish
an eternal relationship with God!

RICK WARREN

Stay on the issue of Christ when witnessing,
not the church, or denominations,
or religion, or theological differences,
or doctrinal questions.
Speak precisely of Jesus, the Savior.

CHARLES SWINDOLL

A TIP FOR TODAY

What if you're uncomfortable talking about your faith? Remember: you're not giving the State of the Union Address—you're having a conversation. And besides, if you're not sure what to say, a good place to start is by asking questions, not making speeches.

A PRAYER FOR TODAY

Dear Lord, let me share the Good
News of Jesus with a world that
so desperately needs His peace
and His salvation. Today, let me share
the message of Your Son through
my words and by my deeds.
Amen

23

NO MORE TEMPER TANTRUMS!

Patient people have great understanding,
but people with quick tempers
show their foolishness.

PROVERBS 14:29 NCV

YOUR temper is either your master or your servant. Either you control it, or it controls you. And the extent to which you allow anger to rule your life will determine, to a surprising degree, the quality of your relationships with others and your relationship with God.

Temper tantrums are usually unproductive, unattractive, unforgettable, and unnecessary. Perhaps that's why Proverbs 16:32 states that, "Controlling your temper is better than capturing a city" (NCV).

If you've allowed anger to become a regular visitor at your house, you should pray for wisdom, for patience, and for a heart that is so filled with forgiveness that it contains no room for bitterness. God will help you terminate your tantrums if you ask Him to—and that's a good thing because anger and peace cannot coexist in the same mind.

If you permit yourself to throw too many tantrums, you will forfeit—at least for now—the peace that might otherwise be yours through Christ. So obey God's Word by turning away from anger today and every day. You'll be glad you did, and so will your family and friends.

THOUGHTS FOR TODAY

When you strike out in anger,
you may miss the other person,
but you will always hit yourself.

JIM GALLERY

Anger is the noise of the soul;
the unseen irritant of the heart;
the relentless invader of silence.

101

MAX LUCADO

A TIP FOR TODAY

No more angry outbursts! If you think you're about to explode in anger, slow down, catch your breath, and walk away if you must. It's better to walk away—and keep walking—than it is to blurt out angry words that can't be un-blurted.

A PRAYER FOR TODAY

Lord, I can be so impatient,
and I can become so angry.
Calm me down, Lord, and give me
the maturity and the wisdom to be
a patient, forgiving Christian.
Just as You have forgiven me, Father,
let me forgive others so that
I can follow the example of Your Son.
Amen

HOW BRIGHT IS YOUR LIGHT?

Then Jesus spoke to them again:
"I am the light of the world. Anyone who
follows Me will never walk in the darkness,
but will have the light of life."

JOHN 8:12 HCSB

ARE you living the triumphant life that God has promised? Or are you, instead, a spiritual shrinking violet? As you ponder that question, consider this: God does not intend that you live a life that is commonplace or mediocre. And He doesn't want you to hide your light "under a basket." Instead, He wants you to "Let your light so shine before men, that they may see your good works and glorify your Father in heaven" (Matthew 5:16 NKJV). In short, God wants you to live a triumphant life so that others might know precisely what it means to be a believer.

104

If you're a believer whose passion for Christ is evident for all to see, congratulations! But if you're plagued by the temptations and distractions of these troubled times—or if you've allowed the inevitable frustrations of everyday life to obscure the joy that is rightfully yours—it's time to recharge your spiritual batteries.

The Christian life should be a triumphal celebration, a daily exercise in thanksgiving and praise. Join that celebration today. And while you're at it, make sure that you let others know that you've joined.

THOUGHTS FOR TODAY

Virtue—even attempted virtue—brings light;
indulgence brings fog.

C. S. LEWIS

If you want to cast a big shadow . . .
stand in God's light!

ANONYMOUS

A TIP FOR TODAY

Find the right crowd and join it. And while you're at
it, avoid people and places that might tempt you
to disobey God's commandments.

A PRAYER FOR TODAY

Heavenly Father, renew in me
the passion to share the Good News
of Jesus Christ. Make the experience
of my conversion real and fresh
so that I might be an effective
witness for You.
Amen

25

EXTREME PATIENCE

Always be humble, gentle, and patient, accepting each other in love.

EPHESIANS 4:2 NCV

ARE you an extremely patient guy? If so, feel free to skip the rest of this page. But if you're not, here's something to think about: If you really want to become a more patient person, God is ready and willing to help.

The Bible promises that when you sincerely seek God's help, He will give you the things that you need—and that includes patience. But God won't force you to become a more patient person. If you want to become a more mature Christian, you've got to do some of the work yourself—and the best time to start doing that work is now.

So, if you want to gain patience and maturity, bow your head and start praying about it. Then, rest assured that with God's help, you can most certainly make yourself a more patient, understanding, mature Christian.

THOUGHTS FOR TODAY

Patience is the companion of wisdom.

ST. AUGUSTINE

Be patient. God is using today's difficulties
to strengthen you for tomorrow.
He is equipping you. The God who
makes things grow will help you bear fruit.

MAX LUCADO

109

A TIP FOR TODAY

God has been patient with you . . . now it's your
turn to be patient with others.

A PRAYER FOR TODAY

Lord, sometimes I can be
a very impatient person.
Slow me down and calm me down.
Let me trust in Your plan, Father;
let me trust in Your timetable;
and let me trust in Your love for me.
Amen

26

PRAISE, PRAISE, AND MORE PRAISE

Praise the LORD. Give thanks to the LORD,
for he is good; his love endures forever.

PSALM 106:1 NIV

THE Bible makes it clear: it pays to praise God. But sometimes, we allow ourselves to become so preoccupied with the demands of everyday life that we forget to say "Thank You" to the Giver of all good gifts.

Worship and praise should be a part of everything we do. Otherwise, we quickly lose perspective as we fall prey to the demands of the moment.

Do you sincerely desire to be a worthy servant of the One who has given you eternal love and eternal life? Then praise Him for who He is and for what He has done for you. And don't just praise Him on Sunday morning. Praise Him all day long, every day, for as long as you live . . . and then for all eternity.

112

THOUGHTS FOR TODAY

**Praise and thank God for who He is
and for what He has done for you.**

BILLY GRAHAM

**When there is peace in the heart,
there will be praise on the lips.**

WARREN WIERSBE

A TIP FOR TODAY

Praise Him! One of the main reasons you go to church is to praise God. But, you need not wait until Sunday rolls around to thank your Heavenly Father. Instead, you can praise Him many times each day by saying silent prayers that only He can hear.

A PRAYER FOR TODAY

Dear Lord, You created the smallest grain of sand and the grandest stars in the heavens. You watch over Your entire creation, and You watch over me. Thank You, Lord, for loving this world so much that You sent Your Son to die for our sins. I will always be grateful for the priceless gift of Your Son, and I will praise You forever. Amen

114

SPIRITUAL MATURITY DAY BY DAY

*Long for the pure milk of the word,
so that by it you may grow in
respect to salvation.*

1 PETER 2:2 NASB

WHEN will you be a "fully-grown" Christian man? Hopefully never—or at least not until you arrive in heaven! As a believer living here on planet earth, you're never "fully grown"; you always have the potential to keep growing.

As a Christian, you should continue to grow in the love and the knowledge of your Savior as long as you live. How? By studying God's Word, by obeying His commandments, and by allowing His Son to reign over your heart.

116

Are you seeking to become a more mature believer? Hopefully so, because that's exactly what God want's you to become . . . and it's exactly what you should want to become, too!

In those quiet moments when you open your heart to God, the One who made you keeps remaking you. He gives you direction day by day. So, give God a few minutes each morning. When you do, He will change the tone and direction of your life.

THOUGHTS FOR TODAY

Every Christian would agree that a man's spiritual health is exactly proportional to his love for God.

C. S. LEWIS

Salvation is not an event; it is a process.

HENRY BLACKABY

117

A TIP FOR TODAY

Never stop learning: Your future depends, to a very great extent, upon you. So keep learning and keep growing personally and spiritually.

A PRAYER FOR TODAY

118

Dear Lord, the Bible tells me that You are at work in my life, continuing to help me grow and to mature in my faith. Show me Your wisdom, Father, and let me live according to Your Word and Your will.

Amen

28

EXTREME TRUST

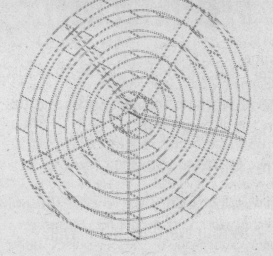

Blessed is he that trusts in the Lord.

PROVERBS 16:20 NIV

SOMETIMES, because we are imperfect human beings who are afraid to trust God completely, we want absolute guarantees before we deliver the goods. But it doesn't work that way. Before we can expect God to work miracles in our lives, we must first trust Him with everything we have and everything we are. Then and only then will we begin to see the miraculous results of His endless love and His awesome power.

120

Do you aspire to do great things for God's kingdom? Then trust Him. Trust Him with every aspect of your life. Trust Him with your relationships. Trust Him with your finances. Follow His commandments and pray for His guidance. Then, wait patiently for God's revelations and for His blessings. In His own fashion and in His own time, God will bless you in ways that you never could have imagined.

THOUGHTS FOR TODAY

If you learn to trust God with a child-like
dependence on Him as your loving
heavenly Father, no trouble can destroy you.

BILLY GRAHAM

Ten thousand enemies cannot stop a Christian,
cannot even slow him down, if he meets them
in an attitude of complete trust in God.

121

A. W. TOZER

A TIP FOR TODAY

In God we trust? You bet! One of the most important lessons that you can ever learn is to trust God
for everything—not some things, not most things
. . . everything!

A PRAYER FOR TODAY

Dear Lord, I will turn my concerns
over to You. I will trust Your love,
Your Wisdom, Your plan, Your
Promises, and Your Son—
today and every day that I live.
Amen

YOUR EXTREMELY BRIGHT FUTURE

*I can do everything through him
that gives me strength.*

PHILIPPIANS 4:13 NIV

LET'S talk for a minute about the future . . . your future. How bright do you believe your future to be? Well, if you're a faithful believer, God has plans for you that are so bright that you'd better pack several pairs of sunglasses and a lifetime supply of sunblock!

The way that you think about your future will play a powerful role in determining how things turn out (it's called the "self-fulfilling prophecy," and it applies to everybody, including you). So here's another question: Are you expecting a terrific tomorrow, or are you dreading a terrible one? The answer to that question will have a powerful impact on the way tomorrow unfolds.

Today, as you live in the present and look to the future, remember that God has an amazing plan for you. Act—and believe—accordingly. And one more thing: don't forget the sunblock.

THOUGHTS FOR TODAY

Life is a glorious opportunity.

BILLY GRAHAM

**There is no limit to what God can make us—
if we are willing.**

OSWALD CHAMBERS

125

A TIP FOR TODAY

Be a realistic optimist: Your attitude toward the future will help create your future. So think realistically about yourself and your situation while making a conscious effort to focus on hopes, not fears. When you do, you'll put the self-fulfilling prophecy to work for you.

A PRAYER FOR TODAY

126

Lord, give me faith, optimism,
and hope. Let me expect the best
from You, and let me look for
the best in others. Let me trust You,
Lord, to direct my life. And, let me
be Your faithful, hopeful, optimistic
servant every day that I live.
Amen

EXTREME WORSHIP

God is spirit, and those who worship him must worship in spirit and truth.

JOHN 4:24 NCV

GOD has a wonderful plan for your life, and an important part of that plan includes worship. We should never deceive ourselves: every life is based upon some form of worship. The question is not whether we worship, but what we worship.

Some of us choose to worship God. The result is an extreme harvest of joy, peace, and abundance. Others distance themselves from God by foolishly worshiping earthly possessions and personal gratification. To do so is a mistake of profound proportions.

Have you accepted the grace of God's only begotten Son? Then worship Him. Worship Him today and every day. Worship Him with sincerity and thanksgiving. Write His name on your heart and rest assured that He, too, has written your name on His.

THOUGHTS FOR TODAY

The most common mistake Christians make
in worship today is seeking
an experience rather than seeking God.

RICK WARREN

129

Worship is our response to the overtures
of love from the heart of the Father.

RICHARD FOSTER

A TIP FOR TODAY

The best way to worship God . . . is to worship Him
sincerely and often.

A PRAYER FOR TODAY

Lord, when I slow down
and take the time to worship You,
my soul is blessed. Let me worship
You every day of my life, and let me
discover the peace that can be mine
when I welcome You into my heart.
Amen

GOD'S EXTREME LOVE

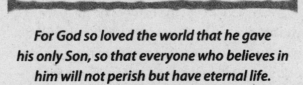

For God so loved the world that he gave his only Son, so that everyone who believes in him will not perish but have eternal life.

JOHN 3:16 NLT

GOD'S love for you is bigger and better than you can imagine. In fact, God's love is far too big to comprehend (in this lifetime). But this much we know: God loves you so much that He sent His Son Jesus to come to this earth and to die for you. And, when you accepted Jesus into your heart, God gave you a gift that is more precious than gold: the gift of eternal life. Now, precisely because you are a wondrous creation treasured by God, a question presents itself: What will you do in response to God's love? Will you ignore it or embrace it? Will you return it or neglect it? The decision, of course, is yours and yours alone.

132

When you embrace God's love, you are forever changed. When you embrace God's love, you feel differently about yourself, your neighbors, and your world. When you embrace God's love, you share His message, and you obey His commandments.

When you accept the Father's gift of grace, you are blessed here on earth and throughout all eternity. So do yourself a favor right now: accept God's love with open arms and welcome His Son Jesus into your heart. When you do, your life will be changed today, tomorrow, and forever.

THOUGHTS FOR TODAY

Our fears for today, our worries about tomorrow,
and even the powers of hell can't keep
God's love away.

BILL BRIGHT

God proved his love on the cross.
When Christ hung, and bled, and died,
it was God saying to the world—I love you.

BILLY GRAHAM

A TIP FOR TODAY

Express yourself . . . If you sincerely love God, don't
be too bashful to tell Him so. And while you're at
it, don't be too bashful to tell other people about
your feelings. If you love God, say so!

A PRAYER FOR TODAY

Thank You, Lord, for Your love.
Your love is boundless, infinite,
and eternal. Today, let me pause
and reflect upon Your love for me,
and let me share that love with
all those who cross my path.
Amen

134

BIBLE VERSES TO CONSIDER

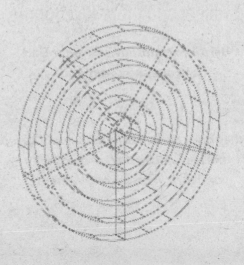

OBEDIENCE

*Those who obey his commands live in him,
and he in them. And this is how we know that he
lives in us: We know it by the Spirit he gave us.*

1 JOHN 3:24 NIV

*You shall walk after the Lord your God
and fear Him, and keep His commandments
and obey His voice, and you shall serve Him
and hold fast to Him.*

DEUTERONOMY 13:4 NKJV

*Here is my final advice: Honor God
and obey his commands.*

ECCLESIASTES 12:13 ICB

*If they obey and serve him, they will spend
the rest of their days in prosperity
and their years in contentment.*

JOB 36:11 NIV

For it is not those who hear the law
who are righteous in God's sight,
but it is those who obey the law who
will be declared righteous.

ROMANS 2:13 NIV

137

ATTITUDE

*There is one thing I always do. Forgetting
the past and straining toward what is ahead,
I keep trying to reach the goal and get the prize
for which God called me . . . .*

PHILIPPIANS 3:13–14 NCV

138

*For God has not given us a spirit of fear,
but of power and of love and of a sound mind.*

2 TIMOTHY 1:7 NLT

*Keep your eyes focused on what is right,
and look straight ahead to what is good.*

PROVERBS 4:25 NCV

*A miserable heart means a miserable life;
a cheerful heart fills the day with a song.*

PROVERBS 15:15 MSG

You were taught, with regard to
your former way of life, to put off
your old self, which is being corrupted
by its deceitful desires; to be made
new in the attitude of your minds;
and to put on the new self,
created to be like God in
true righteousness and holiness.

139

EPHESIANS 4:22-24 NIV

CELEBRATION

Rejoice in the Lord always.
I will say it again: Rejoice!

PHILIPPIANS 4:4 HCSB

At the dedication of the wall of Jerusalem, they
sent for the Levites wherever they lived and
brought them to Jerusalem to celebrate
the joyous dedication with thanksgiving
and singing accompanied by
cymbals, harps, and lyres.

NEHEMIAH 12:27 HCSB

David and the whole house of Israel
were celebrating before the Lord.

2 SAMUEL 6:5 HCSB

Their sorrow was turned into rejoicing
and their mourning into a holiday.
They were to be days of feasting, rejoicing,
and of sending gifts to one another
and the poor.

ESTHER 9:22 HCSB

This is the day the LORD has made; we will rejoice and be glad in it.

141

PSALM 118:24 NKJV

MATURITY

Consider it a great joy, my brothers, whenever you experience various trials, knowing that the testing of your faith produces endurance. But endurance must do its complete work, so that you may be mature and complete, lacking nothing.

JAMES 1:2-4 HCSB

142

Brothers, don't be childish in your thinking, but be infants in evil and adult in your thinking.

1 CORINTHIANS 14:20 HCSB

Older men are to be self-controlled, worthy of respect, sensible, and sound in faith, love, and endurance.

TITUS 2:2 HCSB

Flee from youthful passions, and pursue righteousness, faith, love, and peace, along with those who call on the Lord from a pure heart.

2 TIMOTHY 2:22 HCSB

Now we want each of you to
demonstrate the same diligence for
the final realization of your hope, so
that you won't become lazy,
but imitators of those who inherit
the promises through faith
and perseverance.

143

HEBREWS 6:11-12 HCSB

MIRACLES

Looking at them, Jesus said,
"With men it is impossible, but not with God,
because all things are possible with God."

MARK 10:27 HCSB

I assure you: The one who believes in Me
will also do the works that I do. And he will do
even greater works than these,
because I am going to the Father.

JOHN 14:12 HCSB

But as it is written: "Eye has not seen,
nor ear heard, nor have entered into the heart
of man the things which God has prepared
for those who love Him."

1 CORINTHIANS 2:9 NKJV

For nothing will be impossible with God.

LUKE 1:37 HCSB

You are the God who works wonders;
You revealed Your strength
among the peoples.

145

PSALM 77:14 HCSB

WISDOM

Do not deceive yourselves. If any one of you thinks he is wise by the standards of this age, he should become a "fool" so that he may become wise. For the wisdom of this world is foolishness in God's sight.

1 CORINTHIANS 3:18-19 NIV

But if any of you lacks wisdom, let him ask of God, who gives to all generously and without reproach, and it will be given to him.

JAMES 1:5 NASB

The wisdom that is from above is first pure, then peaceable, gentle, and easy to be entreated, full of mercy and good fruits, without partiality, and without hypocrisy.

JAMES 3:17 KJV

Reverence for the Lord is the foundation of true wisdom. The rewards of wisdom come to all who obey him.

PSALM 111:10 NLT

146

I will instruct you and teach you
in the way you should go;
I will counsel you and watch over you.

PSALM 32:8 NIV

VALUES

Walk in a manner worthy of the God who calls you into His own kingdom and glory.

1 THESSALONIANS 2:12 NASB

148

Therefore, since we have this ministry, as we have received mercy, we do not give up. Instead, we have renounced shameful secret things, not walking in deceit or distorting God's message, but in God's sight we commend ourselves to every person's conscience by an open display of the truth.

2 CORINTHIANS 4:1-2 HCSB

We must not become tired of doing good. We will receive our harvest of eternal life at the right time if we do not give up.

GALATIANS 6:9 NCV

Blessed are those who hunger
and thirst for righteousness,
because they will be filled.

149

MATTHEW 5:6 HCSB

GOD'S LOVE

For God loved the world in this way:
He gave His only Son, so that everyone
who believes in Him will not perish
but have eternal life.

JOHN 3:16 HCSB

For the Lord is good, and His love is eternal;
His faithfulness endures through
all generations.

PSALM 100:5 HCSB

[Because of] the Lord's faithful love we
do not perish, for His mercies never end.
They are new every morning;
great is Your faithfulness!

LAMENTATIONS 3:22-23 HCSB

Help me, Lord my God;
save me according to Your faithful love.

PSALM 109:26 HCSB

Whoever is wise will observe these
things, and they will understand
the lovingkindness of the Lord.

151

PSALM 107:43 NKJV

MY EXTREME DEVOTIONAL NOTES

154

155

156

158

159